Come and Join Us!!!!

We invite you on a journey,
through this New Moments
book series,
to a place where your life will
work so much better!

My friends: Welcome to Volume 1!

CHAPTER 1 – A useful way to think about life

- Mark is stuck ruminating over a relationship that broke down two years ago, spending lots of his moments going over the loss. He also worries that he has not revised at all for an exam that he has known about for six weeks, and it is now only 36 hours away.
- Jean spends much of her days worrying about things going wrong. For example, worries like: *what if something bad happens to a member of my family?, What if I lose my job?, etc.,*.
- Bill feels troubled by not having been as good as he would like to have been with his family (in his life, so far). He also keeps getting upset about blushing in class, last week.

What we focus on and where we direct our attention and energy is crucial in determining how well our life works. Considering the examples, a key question becomes: ***How can we help Mark, Jean, and Bill?***

Before we start developing solutions, let me do a bit of mind-reading! ***If*** you look closely enough, ***then*** most of the moments when you have experienced upset in your life have likely included, either:

(a) going over something that has already happened, in   the very recent or distant past,

<u>**OR**</u>

(b)worrying that something might happen, in the very near or more distant future,

<u>**OR**</u>

(c) perhaps both 'a' and 'b'.

This book can help hugely, with your challenges and the case examples of Mark, Bill and Jean. Firstly, I would like to introduce a way of looking at life which gives us a better platform to make our lives work. I would like you to think of your life as consisting of a long series of moments, represented by the diagram below.

A way to think about your life

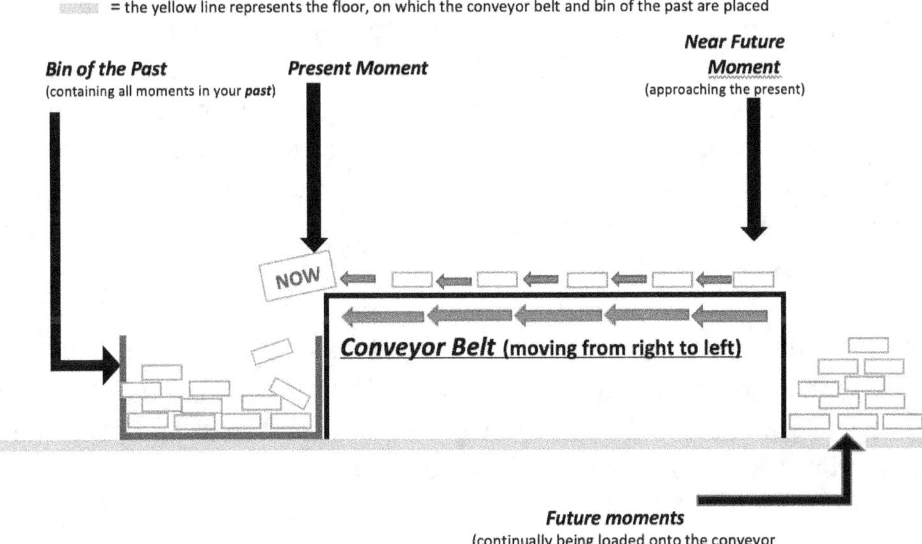

Try to *really* think about this way of looking at things. The conveyor belt moves from right to left (as you look, as shown by the arrows). Imagine that the boxes in the diagram are 'moments' of *your* life (past, present, and future). I know it sounds a bit weird – but go with me on this one!!

By moment, I mean time periods lasting only a couple of seconds. So, the time it takes for you to read *this* paragraph might span three or four moments (boxes on the diagram). By the end of reading this paragraph, the moments involved in reading this paragraph have slipped from the left end of the conveyor belt (i.e., from the present moment; the 'NOW') into the *vast* **bin of the past.**

In life: 'NOW' is all we have, over and over again! The focus is on squeezing as much good as possible out of the 'NOW', over and over again.

At the beginning of the conveyor belt, new moments are being loaded on all the time. These new moments keep being loaded on the conveyor belt, throughout the whole of your life!

Moments which are on the conveyor belt prior to its left end (i.e., ones that have not quite reached the present moment and not quite become 'NOW') represent the very near future. By the beginning of the conveyor belt is a massive pile of boxes, still to be loaded onto the conveyor belt – this is the more distant future. This is unknown, but you can only fully influence it when it arrives in the 'NOW' – over and over again.

Your future and your potential is about how you use these (as yet <u>unused)</u> moments, <u>*when they arrive.*</u> You cannot re-use the old moments which have already dropped into the bin of the past! The *unused* moments are either:

(a) right in front of you (the 'Now', just about to drop into the bin of the past),

OR

(b) further along on the conveyor belt, approaching the now (the near future),

OR

(c) in a massive pile (the more distant future), waiting to be loaded on the conveyor belt - the rest of your life!

Many of people's problems arise from thinking too much about:

(a) **the moments in the *bin of the past* (dwelling on the past).** As an aside, my use of the terms '*bin*' of the past' is *not* meant to disrespectfully indicate that your past is 'rubbish'! Rather, it relates to the idea most people are *less* effective and their lives work *less* well because they over-focus on moments in their

past – which are *gone* and rendered <u>uncontrollable.</u>
and

(b) <u>worrying too much about the moments which are travelling on the conveyor belt or still to be loaded on the conveyor belt (i.e., the future).</u>

In life, **our most precious resource - the key to carving the life path we long for is:** *our time and energy.* A key question becomes:
How will you choose to use the moments which you have, on the remainder of your life journey?

That is:

Where will you put your time and energy in the New Moments?

This is the challenge of designing our life, which is distinct from just unthinkingly continuing on one's current path. Further, *if* **we want to achieve something** *then* **the key is very often focussing our time and energy onto things that we can** *control* **rather than things that we cannot control.**

Psychological science shows that focussing on *uncontrollable* factors (like moments that have gone) tends to contribute to depression, lowers mood, reduces confidence, and is ineffective. In contrast, concentrating more on things we *can* control (like <u>New Moments</u>) is more associated with better mood, lifts in self-esteem, increased effectiveness, momentum, and an improved life situation.

<u>Stop living your life in your 'bin of the past'!</u>
In the absence of a time machine, we <u>cannot</u> control *any* **of the moments from the past.** Taking the 'moments of the past' out of the bin and excessively brooding about them will only negatively

impact the *new* present moments. It is like driving a car whilst excessively focussing on the rear view mirror. We'd be a danger to ourselves and others; less aware of danger, and less able to deal with and appreciate what is immediately in front of us.

Dwelling on the past blunts our tools to deal with and appreciate the present moment. By unhelpfully dwelling on the past, we create and enjoy less in the new moments. This notion is illustrated in the diagram, below:

<u>A way to think about living life whilst focussing too much on the past.</u>

Of course; when something very upsetting happens (e.g., a major bereavement or trauma, or the breakdown of a loving long-term relationship), it is often important and indeed healthy to spend some time grieving for the loss, often including finding the courage to talk about the upset. This grieving may involve a temporary period of upset and reflection on the past and the associated losses, perhaps contemplating moments that have gone (the loss)

and changes for the future. However, people's life quality and achievements are *often* significantly less than they could be, due to:

(a) excessive *grieving* - i.e., thinking excessively about and getting upset over things in the past - moments that have been and *gone*, including every day issues. Often, these moments can be much more quickly and helpfully left behind, in the bin of the past, rather than repetitively ruminated on and brought into the new moments in the present.

(b) worrying over many issues that *might* happen (including everyday things) but also *might not* happen (and often don't happen).

Of course, sometimes we can learn things from thinking about the past and contemplating what we consider to be prior mistakes. However, what people tend to do is:

(i)   waste too much energy focussing on the past,

(ii)   often when they look back, take from the past (in terms of their interpretations): highly negative, unhelpful, and unnecessary messages.

Some people interpret their past unhelpfully almost all of the time, some only a small part of the time, but everyone does it to some extent. Even the most successful and content person on the planet, has scope for further improving messages which they take from their past.

So, your life is improved if you spend less time unhelpfully focussing on the uncontrollable moments which have fallen into the bin of the past. In addition, *you* can work on improving what *you* choose to make your past mean. We can improve this choice by working on *self-talk* (what we say to ourselves and what we believe, in our own minds), which we will cover extensively in volumes four and five.

When we are re-designing our mind and our life path, the most important conversations are often the ones that we have with ourselves (in our own mind)! Our *self-talk* is crucial and it can get better! Improvement in self-talk typically improves and sometimes transforms a person's life.

With the evolution of our ability to use language in the context of aspects of modern society, we have developed a tendency to focus on the past and future *much* more than is beneficial. Clearly, you cannot simply press a switch in your mind and suddenly stop thinking about the past or future and nor would it always be helpful to fully do this. However, there are vital tools in the 'New Moments' book series that can assist us becoming more helpfully focussed in the present.

<u>Stop excessively staring into a crystal ball trying to see your future; start living your life!</u>

In addition to wasting moments dwelling unhelpfully on the past, many people tend to overly think of the future. Of course, planning and having a vision can be of benefit, particularly *if* it contributes to useful *action* rather than being an end point. However, **people often excessively contemplate the future and very often in the form of 'worrying'.**

Stop wasting your moments relentlessly trying to look round corners into the future! Put down the faulty crystal ball and start looking more at what is in front of you here, right now. This notion is illustrated in diagram, below:

<u>When we look too far ahead and worry excessively about what might happen, we are less effective in the present moment - as illustrated in the picture overleaf:</u>

<u>*Key points:*</u>

Some of the main points from this first chapter, include:

(a)   the conveyor belt model of the moments, as a representation of your life,

(b) your most precious resource is your *time and energy*, in the <u>**NEW**</u> (as yet, unused) <u>**MOMENTS**</u>,

(c) your power is how you use your time and energy in the <u>present moments</u> (again and again and again...). The New Moments book series will help with this,

(d)   Strive to choose to use more of the moments within the rest of your life in a positive way, achieving more of the 'good' (based on what matters to you) moments and having less of the unfruitful moments,

(e) your life will be enhanced by concentrating more time and energy on the things you can control and less time and energy on 'things you can't control'.

(f) your life will likely be improved by focussing more on the present moments ('Now'), and less on either the past or on worrying about the future,

(g) the great thing is, if you have not effectively used the moments in the last day, last week, last year, last decade, or even the last fifty years, <u>there are *new moments* coming along the conveyor belt every single second throughout your life</u>!!! A new day brings a whole new set of *unused* moments. You can apply tools from the New Moments book series and begin to use these new moments in a more positive way!

(h) your future choices do *not* need to be defined by your past choices. You can start to make different choices right here, right now! Every new moment is a new opportunity. In any new moment, you can choose to use this opportunity, even right now!

<u>*By reading chapter one, you have taken many steps and perhaps even some leaps, already!*</u>

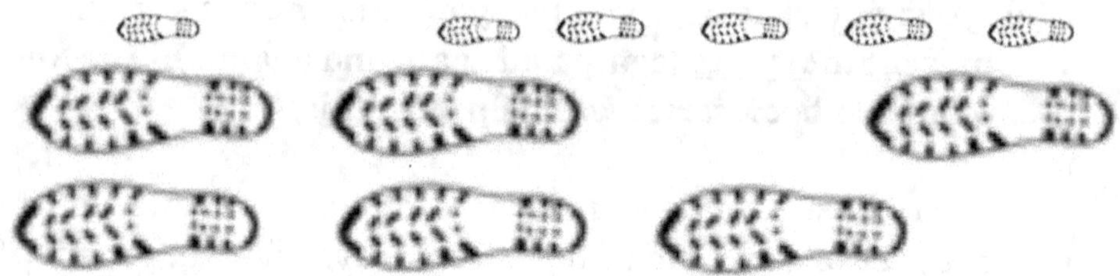

<u>As Lao Tzu advises:</u>

The longest journey in the world begins with one step!

Keep putting one foot in front of other, and one day you may take stock and realise that you have travelled an unfathomable distance!

CHAPTER 2 – You can change your meaning networks, and thereby change your world!

On your journey through the New Moments Book Series, you can change your meaning networks, and thereby change your world! Before that, lets draw from the way of viewing your life which is shown in the conveyor belt model, early in chapter 1. You are reading at this moment, as it sits on the conveyor belt in the present, just about to drop into your 'bin of the past'!

I think you would agree that there are many, many moments which have already fallen into *your* bin of the past. All the moments in the bin of the past represent the whole of your life up to this very moment that you are reading this sentence – *right now*! We are working together, but neither you nor I can suddenly empty this bin of your *past* moments or instantly change the meaning you have given these past moments.

At the point that you pick up this book, you have developed:

- **habits** (repetitive tendencies to respond to certain situations in specific types of ways)
- **meaning networks** [what *things* mean to <u>you</u> (e.g., a social situation, not reaching a target, someone getting angry with you, etc., etc.,.)].

Some habits and some aspects of your meaning networks may be quite helpful. Alongside this, it is likely that some habits and some aspects of your meaning networks will be unhelpful – limiting your achievements and reducing your life quality.

Your current habits and meaning networks have been developed over many years. Even with a very positive system to follow (as is contained within the New Moments book series), changing these habits and personal meaning networks is like a journey. Come with me on this journey through the New Moment book series, and each step can be comfortingly moving you forward and improving your life.

Initially, it is helpful to acknowledge that we *all* view the world through meaning networks. For example: one person's meaning networks may include, *'nobody can be trusted'*, whereas another person's meaning networks may be more aligned with *'there are some wonderful and kind people in the world'*. If we change our meaning networks, we can change what we experience as *'the'* world. If a person's meaning networks are changed, then their world changes!

We will see that the meaning networks which we have, influence the interconnected three things below: **(a)** what we look for, **(b)** the thoughts and emotions which we experience in specific situations, **(c)** what we do.

You will be taught to increasingly influence and choose, what you: say to yourself, focus on, experience, and do. Read on, and you can move beyond the meaning networks which your past has carved, and start to steer your life more.

<u>Take hold of the steering wheel, choose the path, and design your life journey.</u>

******Do not let the past that you did *not* choose control your life path – **increasingly take hold of the steering wheel!**

There are aspects of your meaning networks which are faulty, unhelpful and blocking you from making your life work. This New Moments book series will help you recognise some aspects of your meaning networks which you can usefully change. It will help you through avenues such as: developing useful understanding, encouraging more helpful choices, and assisting with self-talk.

Remember: *Your* view of what appears before *you* depends on *your* meaning networks

***Much of the lenses of our glasses are reflective on the inside, whereby we see implications based on what is already *in our own mind* rather than from an open minded appreciation of *'what is in front of us'.*

Within this New Moments book series, there is extensive coverage of *'self-talk'.* Self-talk (what we say to ourselves about things) can flow from our *personal 'meaning networks* (i.e., our beliefs, assumptions, and ways of looking at the world)'.

Let us take a specific example relating to coping with a set-back. Imagine you have a very good friend, called 'Simon':

*Simon has been sticking to a healthy diet for two weeks, which he has told you is important to him. **If** he then goes out and eats six cream*

cakes, **then** *(in terms of his diet) he has had a set-back!*

<u>INTERPRETATION STYLE ONE:</u>

> **If** Simon unhelpfully labels this set-back in ways such
>
> as **'I am back to square one', 'I have no control',** and
>
> **'it's pointless trying because I always fail',**

<u>then</u>

he is propelled towards **upset, feelings of helplessness, inaction, more set-backs, and defining his future by a past moment.**

<u>IN CONTRAST</u>*<u>: INTERPRETATION STYLE TWO</u>:*

> **If** he helpfully labels that in ways such as **'it's a blip – I have**
>
> **used most of the moments well over the past two weeks',**
>
> **'I am not defined by this blip and it is in the bin of the**
>
> **past – NEW MOMENTS',** and **'let's briefly look at whether**
>
> **I can learn anything from this and then move on – '<u>NEW</u>**
>
> **<u>MOMENTS</u> (the bit I *can* influence and control)",**

<u>then</u>

he is propelled towards **less emotional upset,**
more of a sense of control,
a firmer grip on the steering wheel which
is directing his life journey,
and likely less subsequent set-backs.

The two interpretation styles above reflect examples of *unhelpful* self-talk (interpretation style *one)* and *helpful* self-talk (interpretation style *two).* The past has gone and we strive to approach the present as more of a *blank canvas.* We aim to increasingly hold the brush that paints on this blank canvas. Do not sit back and let difficult parts of our past paint all the pictures in the new moments.

Tell yourself that set-backs or *bad-days* are just that, a temporary and understandable blip, which we can work on and which will pass! Strive to avoid unnecessarily taking unhelpful meanings such as '*I am back to square one*' or '*I can never achieve my goals*'.

If we buy into the latter negative self-talk (e.g., '*I can never achieve my goals*'), **then** it will mean that we are prone to be *de-railed* for longer (at least temporarily). By de-railed, I mean psychologically at a point that we are not helpfully engaged with our life and our goals. That is, not positively engaged in the present (the *new moment*) and 'wasting moments'!!

As our main resource is applying time and energy to the present moments (which are constantly replenished), then: the less we are de-railed during our life journey from this moment forward, the more we use our precious resource of time and energy.

<u>**Remember:**</u> when everyday things are difficult it is often helpful to draw on the idea that when something happens, it **instantly** falls into the bin of the past. Beyond some brief contemplation of whether we can learn anything from something that has already happened, the best focus is typically:

**'NEW MOMENTS' – back to the present and
using the moments NOW, in the best way.**

What is in the bin of the past has gone – do not be unhelpfully hard on yourself for moments that have gone! Where possible, re-focus on and use the 'NEW MOMENTS' and concentrate on **process** (what you do in the new, *as yet unused* moments) rather than what has happened in the bin of the past (**old outcomes**). For some, it may be helpful to use this self-talk 'NEW MOMENTS, RE-FOCUS' in response to set-backs.

We could even visually imagine that set-back moment dropping into the bin of the past, as represented in the diagram at the start of chapter 1. Or, if you prefer, my animator (Jayden Browne) has prepared an alternative representation of the diagram at the start of chapter 1, whereby you are an artist drawing on blank canvases (new moments) which are moving along the conveyor belt (below):

Another way of expressing the Conveyor Belt Moments Model from chapter 1.

A Way To Look At Your Life

The way we deal with set-backs is one of the most important things that determines what we achieve and how well our life goes. In referring to *'how we deal with set-backs'*, I am focussing particularly on: **(a)** *'what we say to ourselves (self-talk)'*, and **(b)** *'what we do'*.

As conveyed in Volume 6 of this New Moments book series: we *can* very often get the most helpful learning (e.g., in terms of mental strength and resilience) from difficult moments rather than the easiest moments. However, this helpful learning only transpires ***if*** we make the right type of choices in these difficult moments and thereby develop the most helpful habits. When we have a difficult moment, the learning often depends on what we paint on the blank canvases which the next *new* moments will present!

So, you have made a great start! You are already half way through Volume 1! It is worth a very brief detour, to touch on the issue of:
How do I best use this New Moments book series to change my life?

Firstly, different people may get different things from the New Moment book series. There are hundreds of ideas or approaches in the many Volumes of this book series. Remember, you do **not** have to understand every point! Every chapter does not have to connect with you, in order for the book to hugely assist *you!* Even if you only take one or two points from the whole series, potentially these points can positively transform crucial aspects of your life!

If things in the book do not seem to fit with you immediately, keep going! **You will get there!** There will likely be big benefits from reading this New Moments book series. The most progress comes from *not just* reading the book, but: ongoingly striving to <u>apply</u> the ideas in this book in many of the remaining *moments* of your life.
<u>**A comical representation of applying the ideas in the book**</u>

In our life journey, we often have ways of looking at and

approaching things which: (a) create *blocks to success* and (b) *increase emotional upset* such as misery, anger, and fear. The *New Moments book series* has helpful ways you can change the way you look at and approach things. It contains tools to create:

- more *happiness*,
- more *success* (i.e., achieving things that matter for *you*),
- Fewer moments of emotional upset within your life,
- more effective use of the moments in your life,

Stop plodding through life! Take the handbrake off and learn how to use a turbo boost! The New Moments book series aims to assist you in overcoming some limits of the human mind.

I am grateful that by reading this book, you are giving me an opportunity to make a positive difference in your life! Lets work on breaking through, together!

<u>You may have blocks between you and your life working....</u>

<u>Do no doubt:</u>
<u>You can use this New Moments book</u>
<u>series to break through!</u>

NEW
MOMENTS
Make Your
Life Work
Love

CHAPTER 3 – Become a winner in life, through changing what you focus on!

In your life to this point, you will have developed habits. One very important set of habits relates to **'what you tend to focus on'**. By *'focus on'*, I mean *'think about'* and *'put your energy into'*. If you try each new day to helpfully change your focus in four key areas, then you will find that you increasingly use your new moments (i.e., **your life!)** in a *much* better way.

To simplify: <u>you just need to make *four* switches to transform your life!</u>

(a) **SWITCH ONE:** Spend more time focussing on what is **controllable** (or at least can be influenced) and less time focussing on what is uncontrollable!!

(b) **SWITCH TWO:** Spend more time focussing on **what you can do** (options which you do have) and less time focussing on what you can't do!!

(c) **SWITCH THREE:** Spend more time focussing on **what is right** about your life and it's possibilities and less time dwelling on what is wrong in your life!!

(d) **SWITCH FOUR:** Spend more time focussing on **what could potentially go spectacularly well in your life**, and less time focussing on what might go spectacularly wrong.

Making the switches does not realistically mean never focussing on the negative side. It means striving to focus on the positive side (rather than the negative side) in a greater proportion of your new moments, from this point on.

By switching focus in these ways, you not only propel yourself to better outcomes and better habits. Making the switches which are suggested will contribute to you being happier, in your life journey.

Your life quality during the remaining steps of your journey (i.e., the experience of the new moments, again and again) will be enhanced by making the four suggested switches! You will also likely switch to having a more uplifting effect on people around you. Attitude is often infectious!

A representation of pushing the four switches (outlined earlier) and the effects of your life:

In terms of **_switch four_**, one is drawing on practical and realistic extensions of 'the law of attraction'. That is, **when our behaviour can influence outcomes**, believing that things will go well tends to make it more likely that things do actually go well. This idea is supported by psychological science.

In areas of uncertainty, making switch four involves living more in what is sometimes termed, positive 'possibility'. Of course, switch four does not translate as suggesting that it is helpful to be wildly unrealistic about things over which we have no control!!

Switch four does not contradict our striving to be present more, in the '*Now*'. Rather, it highlights that in the moments when we do look to the future regarding *uncertain issues*, there is usually benefit in trying to focus on and think more about what things would look like if they went exceptionally well, rather than exceptionally badly. Excessive contemplation of things going wrong tends to drain our energy and contribute to inaction. Switch four includes trying to truly feel and imagine what things going spectacularly well would be like, for you!

Of course, some people might worry *'what if I make switch four and yet things actually go very badly!!'*. We can address this worry in three ways:

a) *Firstly,* making switch four tends to overall enhance our life journey and increase the chances of a positive outcome *in areas where our actions can make a difference*, in the New Moments! Often, ingredients that can help includes growing confidence, but without allowing the growth of unhelpful complacency and inaction.

b) Secondly, a fairytale vision of: *'I will achieve all my goals without any mistakes or failures along the way and there will definitely never be adversity or set-backs in my life'* would be prone to be *unhelpful.* Whilst it would not be helpful to contemplate excessively all the different types of bad things that might happen to us, it would also be unlikely to be beneficial if a person rigidly expected a life without them ever facing any challenges. For many, a positive vision and *switch four* could include: *'I am confident that I could achieve my goals, particularly if I keep going and striving when things go wrong'* and from there, thinking more about the path of achieving the goals than the path of failing or things going catastrophically wrong.

c) Thirdly, this New Moments Book series will give you tools to deal with set backs and things going wrong (including Volume 6). With these tools, you can more sooner bounce back from times when things do go *'spectacularly wrong'*; springboarding to again embracing the new moments with helpful positive focus switches in the beneficial positions. As an aside, some people are helped to deal with challenge by religious faith and the associated meaning.

Question: If something goes wrong for Fred which is very upsetting for him and Fred then keeps his *switch four* jammed onto the negative side (i.e., he is stuck dwelling on everything that might go terribly wrong in his future), *how do you think that will impact his new moments?*

Answer: Switch four being jammed on the negative side will be prone to negatively influence Fred's life, until it is switched back in a New Moment. Switch four jammed on the negative side would *not* promote squeezing everything out of the new moments and neither would it be likely to encourage Fred to be *'going all out'* to create the life and life journey he truly wants.

Of course, making focus switches in more of the new moments can be tremendously difficult and even scary for some people. However, through the New Moments book series, you can develop tools to assist you in helpfully un-jamming switches and achieving more positive focus.

Switch three relates to what has been termed *'gratitude'* or *'counting your blessings'*. Strive to find what is beautiful in your world and the nature around you, in the *'now'*. Look hard for it and you will see more of it!!! Then, focus repeatedly more on that beauty, rather than over-focussing on negative aspects of the world and your past. Remember: <u>we tend to get more of what we look for and focus on.</u>

The value of ***Switch two*** was emphasised within lockdowns associated with Covid-19. In the context of the many restrictions during lockdowns, one had the challenge of trying to focus *'more on what you could do'* and less on *'what you could not do'*. Of course, the Covid restrictions involved challenging adaptation demands.

Switch one is simplified in the subsequent flow diagram, related to tackling many everyday 'problems' (or as I prefer, *'challenges'*). The flow diagram represents a path to using your most precious resource (time and energy) in a more efficient and effective way. It is a practical way of addressing basic problems or issues, to improve how you use your moments in the journey *ahead.*

<u>Flow diagram – Approach problems by making 'switch one', increasing the focus on the controllables.</u>

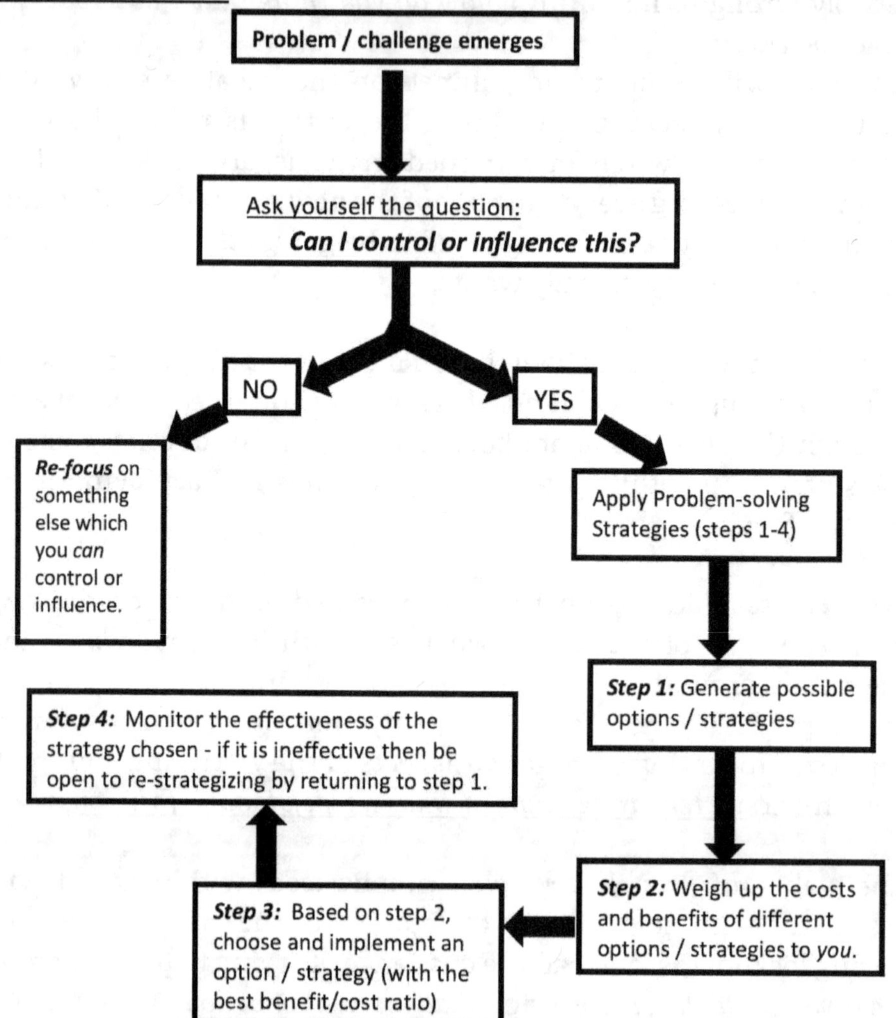

*** The flow diagram is a useful way to approach many everyday type problems and challenges which you might face. By using this approach again and again, you will develop better habits!*
***If a strategy is found to be effective (in Step 4), remain open to the idea that there could still be a better strategy!*
*** The flow diagram works for most things, but when the challenge is a severe trauma, it is often healthy to spend some time gently and gradually contemplating the trauma as part of healing, and often this is helped by discussing it with a trusted person such as a therapist.*

In life, it is worthwhile striving to increasingly focus more on solutions than on problems. The challenge involves:

(a) Working to reduce the gap between: *(i)* dwelling and ruminating about problems, and *(ii)* generating solutions,

(b) Spending less time focussing on problems and more time developing and implementing solutions.

Your life will work better if you can <u>reduce the gap between</u>: (a) seeing and thinking about everyday problems *and* (b) developing solutions. Translating problems into solutions or re-focussing on controllable things can, over time, become like learning a new language – the translation eventually takes less and less time! We start to do it more automatically! You can start to increasingly see the world more as a set of solutions or options, and less as a never ending pile of problems.

Over-time, you can change your habits! You can increasingly make the switches in focus that make your life work so much better. **<u>Whenever you encounter a sense of upset or something you might consider a problem, I invite you to:</u>**

(a) consider what you are focussing on, in terms of the distinctions contained within each of the four switches mentioned earlier in this chapter,

(b) try to make the switch towards focussing more on the helpful aspect (as outlined in descriptions of the four switches at the beginning of this chapter),

(c) if it seems appropriate, use the flow diagram represented earlier in this chapter to navigate your way through to taking positive action,

(d) try to focus more and more energy and thought on *solutions*, rather than excessively ruminating about problems.

(e) be open to asking for help and advice from others.

By going through problems in this way and applying the ideas to your life, you will find that you are making your life work better! More importantly, you will be developing helpful habits and positively changing the *'you'* that comes with you everywhere! These helpful habits will gradually become more ingrained and part of you. This contributes to you feeling more empowered and happier

Case Example: Jerry Coffee.

The self-development specialist, Tony Robbins, mentions that: a man named 'Jerry Coffee' spent over seven years in a 'prisoner of war camp' in dreadful conditions. He was beaten regularly, given very restricted amounts of food, and contained within a small prison cell.

You will see that this case example shows the importance and the power that can come from getting better at:

- **<u>what we focus on</u> (as covered in this chapter)**
- **<u>what we say to ourselves</u> (self-talk, covered later in this New Moments book series).**

Tony Robbins indicates that Jerry was imprisoned along with two other men, who suffered similar maltreatment. Both of the two other men were unable to cope with the maltreatment, suffered terrible upset, and did not manage to bounce back from their experiences as prisoners.

In contrast, Jerry reportedly decided early on during his captivity that: 'if I give up, my life is probably over'. What followed suggests that alongside trying not to give up, Jerry's self-talk may have included questions like:

- *'how can I best use the moments that I have in this massively challenging situation?'*
- *'I know there are lots of things I can't control, but **what can I control**? and let's focus on that' (SWITCH ONE)*
- *'There are masses of things that I can't do, but **what can I do?** and let's focus on that (SWITCH TWO)'*

Jerry also committed to a belief (what he describes as 'faith') that things would work out and he'd get through this and one day be free again (SWITCH FOUR). Jerry then found a way to use moments to focus on some 'controllable factors' (SWITCH ONE) within an environment in which most would likely have viewed themselves as having no control. Tony Robbins indicates that in focussing more on 'What Can I do' rather than 'What Can't I do' (SWITCH TWO), Jerry:

(a) often decided to use a day in captivity to re-live in his mind a day from earlier in his life in massive detail, looking to learn from it in any way. Whilst for most of us this would be 'over-thinking' because we have other options of ways to spend our time, Jerry was adapting to his situation.

(b) managed to do exercises within his very limited space, and became physically stronger.

(c) Began increasingly talking to 'God', which he suggested was facilitated by having nobody else whom he connected with to communicate with during his imprisonment.

There is also evidence that Jerry made SWITCH THREE, in trying to find, appreciate and somehow be grateful for the good things within his environment. This included him taking an interest, fascination, and appreciation of the insects which entered his cell! After Jerry was released from this period of over seven years in captivity, he (Jerry) conveyed that:

*(**a**) he felt he was emotionally, intellectually, spiritually, and physically in a better place than he had previously been at in any other stage of his life!*

*(**b**) he was not bitter or regretful about these specific seven years of his life, in captivity (as an aside, this is consistent with SWITCH ONE, as the past is not controllable).*

I like this story for many reasons, including:

(**a**) it is inspirational and symbolic of what is possible, even in the face of extreme adversity,

(**b**) the story reflects that in a harsh and unstimulating environment, Jerry (partly through his *focus* and his *self-talk*) found a way to positively use the new moments during his captivity!

As an aside, focus and self-talk are inter-linked; getting better at one contributes to improvements in the other. I sometimes use the phrase *'striving to maximise'*, to refer to trying to squeeze as much as possible out of the new moments which we have. Good self-talk and good focus contributes to this *'maximising'*, in life.

On a self-development CD, Tony Robbins states that the difference between Jerry Coffee and the other two fellow prisoners (who had very different and very negative outcomes) was: **'how Jerry communicated with himself (i.e., self-talk) and what he chose to focus on'.** I think that Tony's point is relevant, but not fully inclusive of some important aspects. In particular: Jerry and these other two prisoners likely did not arrive at the beginning of their imprisonments as either blank slates (without pre-existing meaning) or psychologically identical.

In this very moment, all of us carry our own different tendencies towards: giving things certain meanings, patterns of focussing on certain aspects of situations, specific emotional sensitivities, and certain behavioural reactions. In this sense, engaging in positive (helpful) focus and positive self-talk for some people in a given situation may be the equivalent of a brief walk up a small mountain which is not especially steep. In contrast, for others, the mountain may be much steeper and much bigger – due to pre-existing, ingrained and unhelpful *meaning networks* (i.e., ways of interpreting things) and unhelpful habits.

If the mountain that you face right now feels huge and overwhelming, keep going! You can get there, if you come with me on this journey through the New Moments book series. Be gentle with yourself if you fall along the way. We strive to just take one step at a time; before we know it, we have come a long way! The more we climb these mountains and effortfully find positive self-talk and helpful focus switches in difficult situations, the smaller and less steep the future mountains become for us!

As mentioned: we get there, mainly by dealing as best we can with the new moments in the present and right in front of us (now), again and again and again,...and throughout our future! New moments give us opportunities to: *(a)* improve our situation and *(b)* carve out better habits and more helpful meanings and self-talk in our mind. It is straightforward: if we can use more of the *new* moments in a more positive way, then we will make our lives work better! Let' do it!!

<u>*CHAPTER 4 – The value of using 'New Moments'*</u>
<u>*self-talk.*</u>

If we are stuck on unhelpfully dwelling on things that went wrong in our *past* or overly worrying about the *future*, **then** it is likely that life may not feel to be working that well, in this moment! In this chapter, we are looking to use *'new moments'* self-talk to battle with: worrying, negatively dwelling on the past, and associated negative thoughts. By the phrase 'using NEW MOMENTS self-talk', I am referring to using the strategy of:

> ***saying 'New Moments' to ourselves***
> ***and striving to focus on the 'NOW'.***

Let us take ***worrying***. Often, the problems with 'thinking excessively about something upsetting that might or might not happen (i.e., problematic *worrying*)', includes:

(a) we can spend lots of time and energy in dealing with something in our mind, which, when it does *not* happen will mean that time was largely wasted,

(b) even when difficult things do happen, it is often not in the precise way that we foresaw. Remember, we cannot problem solve and fix something that has not actually happened and might not happen – a worry is just in our mind!

(c) it means that many present moments (prior to the issue we are worrying about) are drenched with negative emotion and more unpleasant.

(d) we set up negative expectancies which can sometimes increase the chances of things going wrong (covered in our discussion of 'switch four', from chapter three), particularly in areas where our actions can influence the outcome.

When you find yourself overly thinking *negatively* about the future or the past, the challenge is to use self-talk of 'NEW MOMENTS!'. This may perhaps involve saying loudly in your head ***'new moments'***, as a *re-set* for your mind. Using this latter prompt as a springboard, to concentrate more on getting back to the NOW and creating positive things in the present moment.

For example, *'getting back to being more in the Now'* by creating positively through:

(a) engaging in constructive activity which grounds us more in the 'Now',

(b) making the focus switches covered in the last chapter, such as focussing more on what is controllable.

By doing this repeatedly, *you* are very gradually *re-programming your mind.*

What follows is an abstract example of this living in the moment and controlling the controllable factors. It represents an instance where behaviour could *not* influence the main outcome, but a focus shift could make some difference to the 'Now'. It illustrates an extreme version of focussing in the 'Now', in what must surely be one of the most challenging situations.

Illustrative example:

In an isolated area, a Buddhist Monk slipped off a perfectly smooth vertical cliff face and was heading down a drop of 500ft to jagged rock. The notion is that after falling about 20ft the Buddhist Monk grabbed onto an isolated small tree sticking out of the rock, with nothing else to hold onto between him and the jagged rock nearly 500 feet below.

The Buddhist Monk noticed that this tree was gradually moving out from the rocks and would inevitably give way in maybe two or three seconds, such that he would then continue his fall hundreds of feet to the jagged rocks below. In most situations in life, our behaviour can influence outcome. However, in this extreme instance imagine it was impossible to climb back up this vertical smooth cliff face!

Hence, the Buddhist Monk had only one or two seconds before he continued his fall. In those last few moments, he noticed a beautiful small flower. He was able to enjoy the beauty of this flower in the last couple of moments before the tree gave way and he continued on his fall. I realise that this latter tale may seem unlikely, but I guess it links to this idea that:

> **So often we are focussed on what might be happening in the future or what has happened in the past, rather than fully using or enjoying the present moment!**

Your life will work better if you spend more of your time dealing with **'what is'** (in the present), rather than over-focussing on 'what has been' (past) or 'what might be' (future).

As shown below, you do not have a time machine and so the best approach to life is to spend more moments in the 'Now'.

a
Spend more time in the Now!

Each present moment is like a blank canvas or a blank piece of paper onto which we can paint (create) something. You are an artist, looking to creatively and usefully use the canvas of the present moment (over and over again). By your choices in the present moments, you are painting on this canvas! The aim is to get better at using these blank canvases ('The Now').

Strive to paint pictures that improve your life rather than worsen it! It is worth re-presenting the diagram from chapter 2, below:

Don't over-think the way you have used these canvases in your past. Focus on the new canvas arriving in every moment, now, now, now, now......(again and again). If it helps, then you could visualise the conveyor belt and moments being in (or dropping into) the bin of the past. Using the image to assist in *'letting go'* of moments that have gone and are therefore uncontrollable. What follows is a simplistic and brief soccer example, related to a coach trying to assist a player in getting less bogged down with the past.

Real life case example:

Jonny was a fourteen year old boy practicing long passes of the soccer ball to another player sixty yards away. It was noted by the coach that when Jonny made a couple of consecutive misguided passes, he (Jonny): became very emotional, got more disengaged from the task, became less effective in his passing, and sometimes walked off. The coach, then:

(a) gave Jonny this conveyor belt conceptualisation (chapter one and above),

(b) emphasised his misguided passes were in <u>the bin of the past</u>,

(c) shouted 'NEW MOMENTS' when Jonny's passes were misplaced, which Jonny understood to be re-focus on this new (next) moment.

*The coach also got Jonny to imagine that immediately after a misguided pass, each subsequent pass was more important. In essence, the coach was trying to bring Jonny **back to the present moment**, where his time and energy could make a difference.*

In truth, the next passes after misguided passes are even more important for Jonny because he has an opportunity to carve into his mind: mental strength, useful belief, and an improved ability to bounce back. The latter opportunity is not present in the same way, when he has aced the last five passes.

*The coach also explained to Jonny that how he deals with set-backs will influence mental strength, which in turn will influence his life and career (as covered in Volume 6!). How we deal with 'mistakes, set-backs, and upsets' when they arise will contribute to our future tendencies and habits. Hence, adversity (when things are tough and when things go wrong) tends to present the best **opportunities** for growth and developing resilience!*

*If Jonny has the challenge of a mistake or upset and is more quickly able to constructively re-focus on new moments, **then** his character will be being carved out such that he is more likely to be able to do so in the* *future.*

If we use the present moment well, **then** *potentially the 'mountain that we have to climb' (metaphorically speaking) to use similarly challenging future moments well will become at least slightly smaller. This is really important and will be explained more fully within this book.*

More generally, these ideas apply to other set-backs. So, if we fail an exam and it is important to us to pass this exam, the focus quickly moves away from *the problem* (I failed the exam) to the **solutions** (*how can I get better? - if it is important enough*).

Question: Where does 'a failed exam' *immediately* go?

Yes, that's right, into the bin of the past – 'NEW MOMENTS, we go again!'. Everything that has happened – even a second ago – has dropped into the bin of the past!

We strive to use more of our time and energy (moments) focussed on controllable things to make our life better. For example, doing things to increase our chances of reaching an important goal. We aim to not use our energy to constantly re-live (in our minds) things that have gone wrong, again and again!

We also aim not to take unhelpful messages from the past, but rather we seek to embrace each and every new blank canvas, in the form of the present moment which is gifted to us (over and over again). The messages we take from the past relates to automatic negative thoughts and self-talk; the tools for mastering this area are covered in Volumes 4 and 5.

We strive to spend less time and energy making our life worse by focussing excessively on negative uncontrollable things such as: an event ('failing') which has already dropped into the bin of the past. This latter switch in emphasis can be facilitated by better self-talk. For example, self-talk which promotes:

(a) seeing set-backs as opportunities for learning

(b) judging ourselves more on process (how hard we try and how hard we look for better strategies in this moment, again and again; which we can wholly control) rather than outcome (how we did in any given moment, which has fallen into the bin of the past).

Quiz Questions – Applying 'new moments' principles:

1)　A parent believes that they have not been a good parent to their fifteen year old daughter, but they are scheduled to have a day together tomorrow. On a practical level, if you are this parent, then what is more important: (a) the prior fifteen years of parenting or (b) the day that you are scheduled to spend together with your daughter tomorrow when those moments arrive in the 'Now'? *Clue:* remember 'Switch One' from Chapter 2. Answer is provided at the end of the book.

2)　You play netball for the school team and in all the fifteen games this season, you are convinced that you have not played well. The sixteenth match is on Saturday. On a practical level, what is more important: (a) the match that you have on Saturday when those moments arrive in the Now, or (b) the fifteen matches that you have already played. *Clue:* In terms of our diagrams of the conveyor belt model, where are the last fifteen matches? Answer is provided at the end of the book[1].

3)　You have had six weeks to revise or prepare an assignment homework for school or college. It is now only two days before the exam or assignment deadline and you have done nothing at all in the initial five weeks and five days. On a practical level, what is more important: (a) the five weeks and five days which you have not used, or (b) the two days which you have left. *Clue:* Where will your focus and energy make the most difference, ruminating over what has gone and is in the bin of the past *or* trying to squeeze positive things out of the new moments? Answer is given at the end of the book

Psychological science tells us that focussing on uncontrollable factors (e.g., moments that have fallen into the bin of the past) is not only ineffective, it tends to lower our mood. Spend less time looking in the rear view mirror (at what is in the bin of the past)! Spend less time straining to see negative future possibilities in that crystal ball! Spend more time squeezing all you can out of this moment, right here, right now!

When we are more in the 'Now' (i.e., not focussed excessively on what has already happened and not worrying excessively about the future), we are more likely to be in what is called 'Flow State'. 'Flow state' is a state of mind where we are typically experiencing more pleasure and performing at our best. We can spend more time in the 'Now' by trying to apply the ideas in these first four chapters. In addition, some people find that regularly using basic **'mindfulness meditation exercises'** (e.g., focussed on breathing) can gradually assist in training the mind to spend more time in the 'Now'.

As suggested: following a set-back, we could potentially say to ourselves in our mind, 'NEW MOMENTS'. This can serve as a prompt to re-focus on the new moments and a type of 're-set'. After saying 'NEW MOMENTS' to ourselves, we could perhaps add 'LET'S USE THEM (the new moments) AND STRIVE TO SQUEEZE EVERYTHING OUT OF *THEM!*'.

Over time, through using the positive self-talk and making constructive choices soon after a set-back, it gradually becomes more of a *habit.* That is, it becomes less difficult to use good self-talk and behave constructively following a set-back in our future. We are carving the path to use more of the new moments in a positive way (i.e., carving a path to being de-railed less). Thereby, we are propelled to make our life work better in the new moments, one at a time.

Particularly *if* we have got into the habit of using negative self-talk and not behaving constructively following a set-back, **then** in the early stages, it can be *very difficult* (and take a *lot* of effort) to meet set-backs and still consistently achieve constructive behaviour and positive self-talk. However, the latter 'struggle' and potentially associated upset is not a sign of a problem, rather it is a sign that:

(a) we have an opportunity to grow in a way that will help us make our life work,

(b) we are usefully learning (or re-learning).

The gains in your life from this effortful learning will be HUGE. You are carving helpful habits into your brain!

You are usefully working on perhaps the most precious thing that you own, *yourself!*

This latter position of valuing ourselves brings us to an opportunity to meet a friend – your first companion on this journey. For all the moments where you welcome this friend into your life, they will be there. They can hugely help you, again and again. This friend is *'self-compassion'* and they arrive within Volume 2 of this New Moments book series.

Alongside meeting this friend in Volume 2, you will be helped in putting down some heavy unhelpful baggage which many people carry on their life journey. All will be revealed, in Volume 2!

***Congratulations – you made it to
the end of Volume 1!!***

Volume 2 awaits you!!!

In Volume 2, you can learn how to drop the baggage of blame and enjoy a better life through increasingly snuggling up to self-compassion!

---

[1] Answer to question 1 is: (b). Answer to question 2 is: (a). Answer to question 3 is: (b).

www.ingramcontent.com/pod-product-compliance
Lightning Source LLC
Chambersburg PA
CBHW070230260726

48658CB00006BA/2261